This Walker book belongs to:

_____

_____

_____

For Celia

First published 1986 by Walker Books Ltd
87 Vauxhall Walk, London SE11 5HJ

This edition published 2016

2 4 6 8 10 9 7 5 3 1

© 1986 Shirley Hughes

The right of Shirley Hughes to be identified as author/illustrator of this work
has been asserted by her in accordance with the Copyright, Designs and Patents Act 1988

This book has been typeset in Plantin Light Educational

Printed in China

British Library Cataloguing in Publication Data:
a catalogue record for this book is available from the British Library

ISBN 978-1-4063-7277-9

www.walker.co.uk

THE NURSERY COLLECTION

COLOURS

Shirley Hughes

WALKER BOOKS
AND SUBSIDIARIES
LONDON • BOSTON • SYDNEY • AUCKLAND

blue

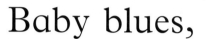

Baby blues,
  navy blues,
    blue socks, blue shoes,

Blue plate, blue mug,
blue flowers in a blue jug.

And fluffy white clouds floating by
In a great big beautiful bright blue sky.

yellow

Syrup dripping from a spoon,

Buttercups,

A harvest moon.

Sun like honey on the floor,
Warm as the steps by our back door.

red

Rosy apples, dark cherries,

Scarlet leaves, bright berries.

And when the winter's day is done,
A fiery sky, a big red sun.

Red and yellow make

orange

Tangerines and apricots,
Orange flowers in orange pots.

Orange glow on an orange mat,
Marmalade toast and a marmalade cat.

Blue and red make

purple

Berries in the bramble patch.
Pick them (but mind the
thorns don't scratch)!

Purple blossom, pale and dark,
Spreading with springtime in the park.

Blue and yellow make

green

Grasshoppers, greenflies,
gooseberries, cat's eyes.

Green lettuce, green peas,

Green shade from green trees.
And grass as far as you can see
Like green waves in a green sea.

black

Shiny boots,
A witch's hat.
Black cloak,
Black cat.

Black crows cawing high,
Winter trees against the sky.

white

Thistledown like white fluff,
Dandelion clocks to puff.
White cover on my bed,
White pillow for my head.

White snowflakes, whirling down,
Covering gardens, roofs and towns.